A Life's Journey Into The Paranormal

Vol 1

Cent The Storyteller

Acknowledgements

First I would like to thank the man in my life. Forever being supportive and understanding. His love through my ups and downs brings calmness in my life as we walk together through the years.

I'd like to acknowledge my family, especially my Eldest Son for his interest, encouragement and enthusiasm moving forward.

To all my Friends and Online community, my deepest gratitude. Years of listening to my story telling, urging me to write my stories and publish a book.

To Cindy, always there with your support and encouragement. When I had my doubts, you would remind me, "You are a writer and author, yet to be published!."

To Silent crow, for your wisdom and knowing's. When I was unsure what stories I should write and what order, you told me, "Start at the beginning." It made logical sense.

To Debs, for your support and unwavering interest. When I had trouble with my writing style you told me, "Write the way you tell your stories to us, Cent."

To Apple, for your heart and understanding. When I struggled glossing over emotion in my stories, you told me, "Bring them to the surface, perhaps bringing closure and healing."

Lastly, I would like to thank my publisher, Writers Clique. The Editorial and Illustration Team as well as the Publishing Department.

Disclaimer

Table of Contents

Prologue 1

1. The Two Boys Next Door............................... 3

2. An Imaginary Friend? 6

3. Out in the Woods... 10

4. Just Call Me Uncle 13

5. A Fishing Lure 17

6. The Mean Little Girl 21

7. The Mysterious Woman............................... 25

8. Whether I see it or not................................ 29

9. An Orange Inside 32

10. Sleep Paralysis... 34

11. The Basement 37

12. This Old Century House............................. 41

13. The Man Upstairs....................................... 45

14. Temporary Lodging 48

15. The Adult Education Centre....................... 51

16. Warp Your Noodle 56

17. Those Bearing Gifts 59

18. A Home of Our Own................................... 62

19. The February Man...................................... 68

20. Their Missing Boy 72

21. The Doctors House..................................... 75

Author's Bio... 80

Prologue

Call me Cent; many of my friends do.

Adults called me timid and shy, a quiet and well behaved child. I was always the last to join in the fun with my siblings, preferring to watch before jumping in. Yet, my funny bone was front and centre around my family, and I loved it when my Dad belly laughed, and his blue eyes would twinkle. For the most part, I had a very happy childhood, smiling and skipping wherever I went. Mom referred to me as her delightful child, nicknaming me Pet.

As with all childhoods, there are also negative aspects of growing up. I was no different. A surviving twin, I was very small for my age and often got teased about just how tiny I was. Often heard, "you're too little to come with us", or Mother calling out to my older siblings to keep an eye on me.

Rarely was I bullied though, with so many older siblings, I was spared that trauma. I was extremely accident-prone as a child, and not just the normal scraps, bumps and bruises. What I'm talking about are freak accidents that one never considers could happen. Like the top portion of my ear cut off, dangling from my head, or the hook of a coat hanger up under my top eyelid. As an older kid, my hand got caught in the rollers of my grandma's old wringer washing machine; it pulled my arm in right up to my elbow. Craziness like that just didn't seem to stop. I often wondered if I would survive to adulthood. No wonder my parents were a little over-protective. I'm surprised they let me out the front door. My poor parents *chuckles*; if a hospital trip was needed, it was usually me.

And then, there is the Creep Factor in my life. You know what I speak of; we've all experienced this at one time or another in our lives. The unexplained or creepiness we encounter. Catching something out of the corner of your eye or feeling you're not alone in the room. The creepiness when the light is turned off, and you run up the basement stairs two at a time. These unexplained events caused me to be easily startled and jumpy at times. Fearful as a child, I would be told there was nothing there and it was just my imagination. I tried hard to believe that.

Then the day came, I realized what I was seeing or feeling wasn't just my imagination. My awareness of this fact hit hard when I was 8 years old.

"Come with me, Dear Readers, on a Journey of Discovery, through the Mildly Amusing, the Unimaginable and Unexplained, to the downright Creepy!"

1. The Two Boys Next Door

I was just 8 years old at the time. We lived in a semi-detached house in the city of Toronto, Ontario. In the house attached, lived an older couple with two small boys. One boy looked slightly younger than me and the other boy was a few years younger still. I never saw them at school, nor were they ever outside playing, not even in their own backyard. Never seeing them leave the house or return from an outing. I remember them looking outside from an upstairs window, never smiling, never waving back. I thought how strange it was that all the neighbourhood kids were outside playing ball, skipping, riding bikes while they would just stand at the window and stare down at us. I felt bad for them.

One night, as I climbed into bed I could hear a "Tap Tap Tap" on the wall coming from next door. I knocked a rhythm on the wall, and they responded with the same rhythm. I grinned at this new found game. We played our knocking game every night for weeks, always looking forward to this small interaction with them.

Then, one night, as I got into bed, ready to play our knocking game, I hesitated. Something was different, something seemed wrong. I placed my hand on the wall, and instantly, I felt a cold darkness and fear I could not explain. Quickly, I pulled my hand away and slowly crawled backwards out of bed. I stood there trembling in the middle of my room, unable to take my eyes off the wall. It felt dark and empty. Terrified and confused, my heart pounded fast in my ears. I didn't know what to do. I wanted to run downstairs to my parents for safety but knew I would be told, don't be silly and go to sleep. Finally, I pulled my bed away from the wall, choosing to sleep on the edge as far away from it as I could. With the wall to my back, I curled into a little ball, pulling the covers around my head peeking out into the darkness, hoping to hear a knock that never came.

I laid there for a long time feeling cold, frightened and alone. Relief came when my tabby cat Fluffy came into my room. Jumping up onto the bed, she gave me a head-butt to my face. I moved the blankets to share them with her, and she curled up in a ball against my chest. I no longer felt so alone as I cuddled and listening to her calming rhythmatic purr, gradually drifting off to sleep.

A few nights passed, and there was no knocking from the other side of the wall. No boys peering out the window. Still scared to be alone in my bedroom, each night on my way to bed, I would call out, "Fluffy, here kitty kitty, puss puss puss". She would come running, bounding up the stairs ahead of me, waiting for me on my bed. I would pick her up and cuddle her, kissing her on the top of her head. "Good Kitty".

Man, I loved that cat, she gave me such comfort. When I was 5, I picked her out of a batch of barn kittens, such a fluffy little fur ball at the time. Little did I know she would grow up to be a short haired tabby cat; I was 26 when she passed.

One evening after dinner, I overheard my parents talking in the living room about the two little boys next door. How sad what had happened. I stood there feeling paralyzed and shocked. To my horror, I found out why the knocking had stopped. The boys died the night I was frightened of the wall. The story was they ingested cigarette butts. I remember thinking, why would they do such a thing? Its craziness! What kid would eat cigarette butts? It didn't make sense; it just didn't make any sense at all! I wanted to tell my parents what had happened to me the night they died, but I couldn't... it would sound like I'm just making up stories.

As time went by, the two boys were no longer talked about. People seemed to forget the tragedy of their demise, past memories of them fading until gone... but I remember them. I will always remember them.

When I think back to that time so long ago, I still wonder what really happened that night to

"The Two Boys Next Door."

2. An Imaginary Friend?

You often hear of children having imaginary friends. I suppose there are many reasons a child has one, and for the most part, make believe is considered a normal and healthy part of childhood. Then again, perhaps sometimes, it's more than imagination.

As far back as I can recall, I noticed a small boy would appear on occasion during quiet alone times. At first I didn't interact with him, just aware he was there. I would see him in my peripheral vision, and yet when I turned to look at him, he would vanish. Gradually, he would reappear, and I would see him again in my side vision. I started to learn I can't see him when I looked straight at him. I began getting very good at using side vision. It became second nature to me at a very young age when children's peripheral is not as developed as adults.

Throughout my childhood, he was growing up with me. He was always the same height I was, ever changing to an older child alongside me as I matured. I began to interact with him more and more. At first, it was small things, were I would say hello with a smile. He would respond with a smile and take a step closer.

It wasn't long before he would appear right beside me, always on my left side. I didn't actually talk to him a whole lot, but felt a connection to him that words weren't needed. I would include him in play or sometimes he would just sit and watch me make sandcastles by the lake up at the cottage.

Sometimes, if I was being scolded, he would stand slightly behind me on my left. Teasing me, he would shoulder bump me as he giggled. Turning my head slightly to see him, I would whisper, "Stop it". Of course, Mother would then scold me for not paying attention. He would burst out laughing; it was all I could do not to giggle, knowing I would be scolded for not taking the situation seriously.

I remember the year my Dad re-vamped one of my older sibling's bikes they had grown out of. He spray painted it, added curly q handle bars with streamers, and a banana seat to boot. What more could you want from a ride that gave you so much freedom? Being a Big Kids bike and me being so tiny for my age, he lowered the seat as low as it would go and added 2 training wheels to help. I practiced and practiced, so Dad took off one training wheel. He laughed and told me to head for the grassy boulevard if I was falling.

Back in those days, bike helmets weren't a thing. In no time at all I wasn't relying on the remaining training wheel and was using it more for a kickstand than anything else. So Dad removed that one as well and added a real kickstand to my bike. Finally, I was riding a big kid's bike like the rest of the neighbourhood kids and my friends.

One early morning I decided to hop on my bike and take a tour all by myself around the neighbourhood. As I mounted my bike, the boy appeared beside me so I moved up on the banana seat to make room for him. He sat behind me as I pedaled faster and faster down the hill. In a split second decision, I pulled my feet away from the pedals, knowing the only way to stop the bike is to peddle backwards to apply the brakes. It was thrilling, exhilarating, and scary all at the same time!

I glanced to my left, and the boy had his chin on my shoulder and his arms stretched out, grinning as the wind whipped past us. Slowly I put my feet on the pavement to slow us down and regained control of the spinning pedals. I gently applied the brakes and came to a full stop.

Out of breath, adrenaline pumping, and still feeling the thrill of the ride, I started to giggle. He joined in, and we both started laughing like a pair of hyenas. I didn't tell anyone about my thrill ride, even kept it from my siblings for fear they would tattle to Mom and Dad. My freedom and new bike would have been taken away for at least a week for taking such a risk... but it sure was fun.

Birthdays were emotionally confusing to me as a child. I would become quiet and sad a few weeks before and up to my birthday. Mom would say, "Why so glum, chum, it's your Birthday, be happy!" It was enough to snap me out of it, returning to my happy self. It wasn't until I was a teenager that I put 2 and 2 together. I was sad and missed my twin brother.

He was born a few weeks ahead of me and died before I was born. The powers that be took him from me, not allowing us to be together in this mundane physical world. Resentment and sometimes even survivors' guilt was very much a part of my life. I knew in my heart my imaginary friend was actually my twin brother.

As my childhood ended and the fun and games stopped, he appeared less and less. I no longer looked forward to his arrival like when I was a child. For you see… he only appears when something traumatic was happening or was about to happen. I find it curious he grew up to be a young man and yet never aged alongside me as an adult.

So, the next time you hear tell of or witness a child pretending to play with an invisible friend, you must ask yourself. Is it really just…

"An Imaginary Friend?"

3. Out in the Woods

From the cottage, we went on a trip farther north, up to the Canadian Shield. Granite mesas and giant evergreens lined the small highways. It is a land of lakes and rivers, truly nature in its glory. Turtle, Deer and Moose crossing signs were common along the roads. I enjoyed seeing the animals and birds and looking for the beaver dams and lodges along the way. I loved the wilderness and couldn't wait to get out of the car to explore.

We traveled up north often, as my Mother had a lot of kin in that area. This trip it was for an elder's 50th wedding anniversary, and many were gathering. We all met up at the town's old community hall up on the hill, just on the outskirts of downtown. You could almost see the whole town from that vantage point.

A spread of many bowls and plates of food lined the tables, with many deserts. A special cake was on a separate table. After dinner the ladies packed away the food and cleared the tables as the men gathered the garbage and rearranged the room for a dance floor. I decided I best go to the rest room before the next phase of the party began. I went to my Dad to let him know, and he gave me a flashlight. It was already dark and I would need it to navigate the gravel path and to see inside the outhouse.

Walking along the path, the gravel made a quiet, crunching sound under my feet. Looking up, you could see small brown bats in the moonlight, swooping above me in the tree tops, feasting on insects. The gravel ended at the outhouse, but I noticed a small trail continued farther, weaving through the trees. Shining my flashlight down it, I could tell it went a long way into the woods.

Checking for spiders and webs first, I hung the flashlight on the hook on the door and went about my business. My mind wandered, thinking, if it was still light out, how cool it would have been to walk the small trail to find out where it led. Grabbing the flashlight and unlatching the door, I heard something. Someone... or something was coming down the trail out of the woods towards the gravel path.

Startled, I quickly re-hooked the door and turned off the flashlight. I peeked out the crescent moon cut out in the door but couldn't see anything down the dark trail. Sticks and twigs cracked louder as it approached the gravel path, but then, it stopped. I froze and held my breath, straining to hear movement, all the while telling myself to be calm; it was probably just a deer or raccoon. Worry began to creep in, what if it was a black bear? My heart began to race, and adrenaline pumped through my body; there was no way I could outrun a bear.

It took me forever to find the courage to leave the safety of the outhouse. With shaky hands, I quietly unlocked the door and cracked it open. My eyes darting back and forth, I silently crept out closing the door gently behind me. I stood like a statue against the door for a few minutes as I scanned the area for movement. Slowly I started walking backwards in the dark, down the gravel path, back to the hall, back to safety. Almost halfway there, my eyes caught a shadow move. Jump startled, I quickly turned on my flashlight in the direction of the movement!

Peeking around a tree was the face of an older man staring back at me. He looked weathered with his eyes and cheeks sunken, unshaved and unkempt hair. Where was his body? The tree was to small to hide behind! Fear took over, and I began to shake. He wasn't from our party...I was overwhelmed and scared ...Time to Run! I spun around and took off down the path!

Ahead of me, I could see my Dad standing at the end of the path. I'm not sure just how long he was standing there before I noticed him. Slowing down to a fast walk, I turned and shone the flashlight behind me. The face had disappeared into the woods. My Dad said, "Are you alright? I wondered what was keeping you."

Grabbing his hand and looking up at him, I replied, "I got scared of the bats swooping down." I don't know why I lied to conceal the truth. There were lots of ghost stories and I had heard the tales of the old man in the woods. Until now, I thought that was just to scare us from wondering off and getting lost. Was that the old man in the woods? But there was something off about him. Were my eyes playing tricks on me? Was it simply a case of pareidolia? Shaking and confused, Dad took the flashlight from my hand and shone it down the dark path. Turning to look, we both stood there for a few minutes, staring down the gravel pathway. He knew it was something more than bats that had frightened me.

Squeezing my hand to come along, he said, "It's important to keep your wits about you because you never know what you might come across"....

"Out in the Woods."

4. Just Call Me Uncle

In my early-teens, tragedy struck our family. Most of the summers were spent at the boat or the cottage with my grandparents. Dad would drive up from the city on Friday nights after work to meet us at the lake for the weekend. It's a generational piece of property, cozy and felt like a second home.

One evening, as we kids played checkers, crokinole and read comics, our parents and grandparents played cards in the summer kitchen. I heard Mom exclaim, "Oh look, someone's pulling in the driveway... it's a police cruiser!" I got up and moved towards the door; my Mother appeared in the doorway and sternly said, "You kids, stay here!" I resisted the urge to sneak out into the back kitchen to see what was happening.

As I stood there waiting, my twin appeared beside me, putting his arm around my waist. My heart began to pound in my chest; I knew something was terribly wrong. I heard my grandmother outside start screaming; it shook me to my core. I heard the chaos come crashing through the door into the back kitchen. Suddenly, everything went silent; the only sound was the blood rushing through my ears. There was a stillness that hung in the air. It was like there was a barrier surrounding me as I stood in the middle of this... bubble. I watched as my grandmother entered the room, pulling at the curls on top of her head, handful after handful, Mom and Grandpa reaching, grabbing her wrist and arms to stop her. Everyone's mouths were moving, but I couldn't hear what they were saying. I looked at my sibling's faces contorted as they cried. I was confused and stood there dumbfounded as to what had happened. Grandpa ushered Grandma to their bedroom as Mom approached me. She reached out and held my hand. The reaction was immediate I could hear everyone crying. Mom gently said to me, "Uncle has died in an accident."

I was shocked, horrified and numb all at the same time. I just stood there in disbelief, crying silently. I closed my eyes, allowing the tears to stream down my face. Seeking solitude, I went outside and watched the police car drive away. My twin brother never left my side.

I'm not sure what had happened. Did my mind shut down as a response to my grandmother's screams? An emotional shutdown? Was my twin brother the cause, trying to shield me from it as he tried to comfort me? I can't really say for sure.

Sleep came late that night, listening to the murmurs of the adults talking in the living room. Morning came and we ate a silent breakfast as the adults packed and loaded the cars up. Arrangements needed to be made. It was a long, quiet trip back to the city; each person emerged in their own thoughts. I learned he died instantly on his motorcycle, in a head on collision with a large truck.

The funeral was difficult, and they closed the curtains a couple of times to fix my uncle. A lot of chest damage from the handle bar of his bike. They finally closed the casket and a minister said blessings and drew a cross with oil on the lid. An unknown man stood up and swiped his fingers through the oil a few times. My Mother was startled in her seat and became visibly upset. I think my Mom had the minister pour more oil on his casket afterwards. After the funeral our house started feeling heavy, some areas feeling like the air pressure changed when I walked through it. Thinking it was the sadness everyone was feeling, I tried hard to ignore it.

We had moved to a single family back split home a few years back, and I had recently given up my bedroom so my two little sisters didn't have to share. I loved being in the back lower part of the basement. Had my own couch and chair, my aquariums, my own little sanctuary. It was great. But then, I started to feel I wasn't alone in my room; I would squeeze my eyes closed as I fought my fear to run. Slowly, I would make my way up to the main basement, then up the long flight of stairs to the lower main level. This presence grew stronger and stronger. In my mind, I could see a man standing behind me. I was to frighten to turn around and look, in case it was true. My fear started to escalate, and I would often walk up the stairs backwards, trying to stop the creepiness that I was being followed.

One afternoon, when I was down in my room feeding my fish, I felt the room change. The heavy feeling when the air pressure changes surrounded me. You know, like when the barometer drops as thunderstorms move in. Feeling that strong presence behind me, I froze and stared at the chrome hood of the fish tank, looking to see if I could catch a reflection... a glimpse of what it was. I saw a shadowy movement behind me. I shivered as goose bumps raised the hair on my arms. "Don't run, don't run!" I whispered to myself. My heart began to race.

I caught more movement in the reflection of the chrome hood; it was very close, standing right behind me. Suddenly, I felt someone gently put their hand on my shoulder! Gasping, I went into full panic mode! I raced out of my room and flew up the stairs two... three at a time, closing the basement door behind me! Standing there, I held the door closed and tried to settle the tremors coursing through my body. In the distance, I heard my Mother say something from the kitchen. Not wanting to be alone, I decided to join her. I went up the few steps to the foyer and could see my mother in the kitchen by the sink. She was bent over, hands covering her face as she sobbed. I heard her say in a pleading, desperate tone, "I can't do this anymore. Please... please, you have to leave." My jaw dropped. Stunned, I crept silently back down to the family room.

Understanding came; she was talking to her brother, my uncle. After all these years, why didn't she believe me when I was scared? It wasn't until I had my own children that I felt I understood. Perhaps, in her own way, she was trying to protect me from such things. If not talked about, it doesn't exist, plain and simple.

I never felt or saw him after that. Over time, the house became a happy place to live in once more. There are a lot of fond memories that stayed with me. He'd take me for short spins around my town on his motorcycle when he came to visit. He had won many trophies for car racing; my mom kept them and placed them on the shelving unit in the family room.

I would always call him by his full name; he would joke and turn with a smile, saying,

"Just Call Me Uncle."

5. A Fishing Lure

When I was little, Dad had a small Cabin Cruiser. It was a great boat for water skiing and fishing. Sometimes, we'd go swimming in the deep waters or go to the sandy shallows near one of the islands. It wasn't long before our family grew and it was getting cramped, time for a bigger boat. Dad, being a master carpenter, decided to build his own boat. He selected the plans and went about erecting a temporary building beside the cottage to house the boat, while it was being built. The interior design was set up for dual purpose, day and night. All the seating was designed to drop down to double beds or pulled up to create bunk beds.

He ordered an engine from England to power the propeller, stating he needed it to handle extra weight since we could now travel. It had plenty of room for sleepovers and, of course, so we could still waterski. Man, that boat could move; the bow would come up as we skimmed across the water. Not many Houseboats can move like that. You heard me correctly, a houseboat. My parents decided to name the boat *Knot-a-Buoy*, a play on words since they had six daughters. When we traveled the Trent Canal, the Lockmasters would chuckle when they got the joke.

We often went over to the cottage via water with our new boat to visit with grandma and grandpa and to play on the sandy beach. On one of those visits, the next-door neighbour had caught a huge fish, he had it laid out on his picnic table to clean it. It was so big its tail hung over the edge. At first, I thought it was a

Northern Pike, but it was much too large. So I asked, "What kind of fish is that?"

"A Muskie," he replied. I had thought the biggest fish with teeth was a pike, but boy, was I wrong. There are many stories of the deep waters in this lake; for me, Muskie was now added to this list. *Note Muskie fishing is no longer allowed in Lake Simcoe, was it because of over fishing or… one of the Serpentine Legends that dwindled their numbers? Let me share some of the Legends with you.

At the southern end of the lake, there is the Cook's Bay creature, said to be charcoal coloured and scaly. Many say it's extraterrestrial. In the 1970s, I remember many were talking about UFOs entering the water on the eastern shores, there are still reports to this day.

The Serpentine Legends are many, our very own Loch Ness Monsters. Indigenous people of the region called it Mishepeshu, a horned sea serpent with the head of a dog. Back in 1823 started the Kempenfelt Kelly sightings. Today, we call it Igopogo, The Monster of Lake Simcoe.

Well… Dad decided he was going try his hand at landing a Muskie. He bought the weirdest fishing rod I had ever seen; it was very short with a big real. Instead of a heavy test line, it was a metal cable. It made me realize just how strong its jaws and teeth were. He used a huge spinner with brightly coloured streamers as a lure and added a significant weight to ensure the lure went down deep. Utilizing the lake map and our depth finder, we located where the deeper parts of the lake were. I got to Man the Helm in the open waters as Dad trolled for a couple of hours without success, not even a bite. I was disappointed for Dad but also a little relieved.

The wind started picking up, and the water was getting choppy; I slowed down to a float while Dad reeled in the line. A storm was coming, and that lake could get dangerous very quickly. As we all battened down the hatches and gathered the towels, a gust of wind grabbed one of my mom's new bright pink bath towels and into the drink it went. It floated for just a minute and started to sink. Mom motioned to my older siblings to jump in and get it, and they all chickened out. Without hesitation, I took the deepest breath I could and leap dived off the boat!

Down I swam, trying to catch up to the towel's descent. The water was becoming very cold, and the dark abyss below me was frightening! Reaching out to grab it and missing, two more frog strokes and I was able to grab it. Slowing and stopping my descent was more challenging than I thought; the towel was very heavy.

As I headed for the surface, I slowly began to exhale as I ascended. I couldn't help but imagine a huge fish or serpent coming up out of the depths, mouth open, chasing me. After all, Dad had just been trolling; what if something was following his lure? I started to panic when, all of a sudden, I was no longer inside myself. I was outside myself, watching me struggle to reach the surface! Confussed, how can I be watching myself?

Without anything more to exhale, my lungs began to scream to take a breath. I became aware of myself again. Seeing my family looking down at me from above gave me hope. I hit the water's surface, gasping for air; my body felt numb and weak. Grabbing the lowest rung of the ladder, I held the towel up, and

Dad reached down and grabbed it. Seconds later, he reached down and grabbed my wrist, pulling me straight up out of the water and onto the deck. He was grinning at me and said, "You okay?"

Gasping and nodding at him, I replied, "Next time, buy a new towel or at least try not to look like..."

"A Fishing Lure!"

6. The Mean Little Girl

I was the youngest of four children for 10 years until a wonderful thing happened. My parents were blessed with a baby girl. Two years later, another baby girl was born. They were adorable with their giggling and play, exploring their world. Like living dolls, they were all dressed up in pretty clothes with bows in their hair. It was fun helping them learn to crawl and walk. What was really great? I wasn't the youngest anymore; I have two baby sisters! By the time I was 17, it was only the three of us living at home. The rest of our siblings had flown the nest.

I started noticing people tended to have many different types of what I call Natural Human Abilities. I believe everyone has them, our extra senses; some call them gifts. How do we know there is danger when our eyes see no signs of it? Or when you're thinking of someone and they call you or stop in for a visit? Nature and animals have this as well; we usually call it instincts, part of the genetic code. It's built into our DNA. Many will deny such things until these abilities fade into the background, but children are an open book.

When my little sisters were 4 and 6 years old, I noticed each of them had certain pronounced abilities. My first little sister could produce answers to questions she couldn't possibly know about. It was like she pulled the answers out of thin air. To this day, if you're playing Trivia Pursuit, you want her on your team. When asked, how do you know? She would say… "I just guess!"

My youngest of sisters enjoyed guessing games, being incredibly accurate with a deck of cards. She started guessing colours red or black, but then after a while she started being able to tell you the suit and eventually the card number as well. She also had an uncanny ability to announce when someone was about to show up at our house unexpectedly. I thought it was pretty cool, although not everyone felt that way.

My ears perked up one day when I overheard my parents discussing baby sister had an imaginary friend. Now, I never spoke much about my twin brother, I kept him a secret, knowing it would be downplayed as imagination. My baby sister, however, spoke out loud about this imaginary friend. Talked like she was a kid from next door that came over to play. Adamant, she would argue... "She is Real!" When she was 5 years old, things began to escalate.

Baby sister's bedroom was right beside the main bathroom upstairs. One weekend, after my shower, I could hear her talking. Her door was cracked open, so I peeked in. How cute! She was having a tea party, with little chairs all around her table. An extra chair had a doll and a little rocking chair that sat empty.

"Some for you, Dolly. Would you like some too Katie?" She said, pouring water into the teacups. At that, the rocking chair tilted slightly forward and held that position. A few seconds later, it moved back to its original position!

Needless to say it was a Startling and Creepy Holy Crap Moment; I had never witnessed an object move like that before. I couldn't see anything in the chair but I now knew there was more to this imaginary friend than meets the eye. As I left, I heard her voice change and become angry. Turning around, I headed back up the stairs; without knocking I opened her door quickly. "Is everything okay in here?" I asked.

She looked up at me and smiled, "Yes, I'm okay," her room had a heavy feel to it.

I smiled back at her and said, "Just checking," and headed to my room in the basement. I gave it some thought and decided if she's happy, it's all good. Boy, I was so wrong. Her life became very turbulent; she was no longer a happy little kid. She was getting in trouble a lot, refusing to listen to reason and blaming Katie for things. I remember one evening after dinner, I witnessed her running down the hall and getting pushed from behind. She went down hard; up the stairs, I ran.

As she picked herself up, she said, "That wasn't nice." Squatting down beside her, I asked if her knees were okay. It was then that I saw her in my peripheral vision; I saw Katie. She stood in the middle of the hall; her dress was just below her knees, very old-fashioned. Her hair down past her shoulders, she appeared to be a little older than my sister.

I asked my sister quietly, "Tell me, what does Katie look like?"

"She's tall with long brown hair and a long dress," was her reply, and off she went into her room as if it wasn't a big deal.

I had no idea what I could do to stop all this crazy. My little sister was being bullied ... I didn't like it. Standing up I firmly said, "I know you're there, I can see you. Leave my sister alone!" I watched as she gradually faded from the hallway. A few weeks passed by with little change in the situation. A terrible argument broke out; this was the last argument about Katie. She was no longer talked about, but slowly over time, my little sister was a happy little girl again.

Katie was gone, only the memory is left of...

"The Mean Little Girl."

7. The Mysterious Woman

What a beautiful day on the boat! The lake was like glass, perfect for water skiing and swimming. Later in the afternoon, that all changed, a storm was moving in fast. Headwinds were strong, in less than half an hour, the sky turned black and angry. Dad decided it was safer to head through the narrows into Lake Couchiching and dock at the port. It was much closer than trying to make it to the cottage or marina before the storm hit. Lake Simcoe is notorious for major storms sweeping in. I remember when I was very young, watching the sky turn green and a water funnel moving across the lake, entering the cove at the cottage. We all ran into the cottage for shelter; as the wall of water hit, the building groaned and shifted. The aftermath wasn't too bad, except for the fish we were trying to save.

We had to fight the wind and waves to the narrows between the two lakes, just as we entered, the storm hit with brute force. The torrential rain made it difficult to see as we followed the beacons of lights into the port. Dad made several approaches to line up with the cement docks along the shore each time the wind and water tossed us around like a tub toy. Two of my older siblings were on deck, one on the Bow and the other on the Stern, with hooks at the ready to pull the boat up tight to the dock so we can tie it down. Dad lined us up on the Port side *left* and they were able to hook the dock and jump off, ropes in hand. The boat tossed up and down, in and out, smashing against the cement dock. Bumpers doing little good being pushed up from the churning, heaving water. Dad manned the wheel fighting to keep the boat in place so they could secure us to the dock. All of a sudden, the bow pitched downwards and sprung back up, yanking the rope from my sister's hands.

I ran up the stairs from the safety of inside and out onto the Bow. The Bow bobbed and swung out as I grabbed the rope, water sweeping over the bow each time we dipped down. Through the rain, I could see people running towards the dock to help us. An image flashed in my mind of my twin brother. I threw the rope to my sister, and then darkness enveloped me. I have no memory of the accident or my legs being crushed; I was wedged between the boat and the dock. Either I lost consciousness or my brain shut down during the trauma. I was later told it was my father who saved me, pulling me up and out of further harm's way.

Awareness came, and I could feel the rain on my face; I was in the stairwell, my Mother sitting behind me, holding me tightly. My left leg was numb, and my right leg was on fire! I tried to look down at my legs, but my Mother grabbed my chin, lifting my head up and holding me firm, not allowing me to see. I went into panic mode, struggling and fighting her. I began to scream, "Don't let them take my leg! Don't let them take my leg!"

I think I passed out because when I became aware again, the rain was no longer pelting me in the face. I opened my eyes to a blue sunny sky above me; we were in the eye of the storm. I tried to move, but Mom was still holding me firm. In the distance, I could hear sirens. I noticed a woman was on the deck, standing behind us.

Dressed all in blue, she was absolutely stunning; her skin looked like porcelain, with large, bright blue eyes and hair so black it shone blue in the sunlight. Smiling at me, she leaned over and gently said, "You are going to be alright." Nodding, she repeated, "You are going to be alright." I completely believed her as I drifted off into darkness. I'm told my Dad carried me off the boat and into the ambulance. A faint memory of the ride to the hospital, I was worried we'd be in a car accident going through a red light. Darkness swirled me into oblivion yet again.

I came to in the Emergency Room, my leg burning. I looked down; they had loose coverings over my ankle, and my foot was cold and very pale. As I wiggled my toes, the blue lady's words ran through my mind. My parents came into the room; their faces showed worry. Not wanting to hear any bad news, I asked, "Who was the lady on our boat?" Mom looked confused and asked me what lady I was talking about. I continued, "The lady standing on the bow of the boat with us, the lady dressed in blue."

Mom looked confused and glanced to Dad. She shook her head, and told me, there was no one else on the boat. I was adamant that there was, describing what she looked like. There was silence for a moment, Mom finally spoke telling me that perhaps it was my guardian angel. She smiled with reassuring gentleness. I laid there confused, did I imagine her? No one else saw her. We waited in silence for the doctor to return.

Just as my parents and the doctor stepped outside the room to discuss my injuries, the Emergency Room became chaotic. I looked out the doorway and saw a man dripping wet, his face distorted in panic. In his arms was a small boy, limp and soaked.

The man was Screaming for help, yelling my son fell into the water. There was a frenzy of emergency personnel swarming the area. It was very unsettling. Hours later, I learned the little boy had died, he drowned at the same dock, the same area, where I had my accident. This news haunted me. Why? Was there something wrong with the area? Was it supposed to be me? It couldn't be just a coincidence. It stuck in my mind and remains in my mind all these years. Poor little guy... and for the parents the death of a child is unbearable. That kind of loss rips your heart out of your chest. Something I myself would experience decades in my future.

It was a long road to recovery; physical therapy was difficult, and I hated the ice packs. Aside from a tiny bone fragment working its way out of the wound, miraculously in time, the rest of the bone fragments fused back together. Left with a nasty scar above my ankle and a dent in my leg, I was very lucky. There was no need for pins or rods, and I healed well. I had no doubt in my mind I would walk again normally with no limp. I just knew I was going to be okay.

I'm still not sure just what or who she was but I believed...
"The Mysterious Woman."

8. Whether I see it or not

I had always wished, I couldn't see things others didn't. I started to wonder if there was something wrong with me. It got so; I just didn't say anything because people would look at me like I had lost my mind. I tried hard to hide my emotions and body language. There was no group or outreach program I could turn to, no Internet. Back then, the only books available were from a handful of authors hand-picked by publishers. I found no answers to the many questions I had. Alone with my own fear, my go-to was trying to pretend it wasn't there or to simply leave the area. Then, something happened that changed my mindset.

It was at a Christmas Party, a buffet-style dinner, that I witnessed something that changed my mind about seeing things. I knew most of the people, but it was work-related, and being one of the youngest adults at the party, I felt somewhat on my own. The spread of food was impressive. I filled my plate and went and found a chair to sit on and eat my dinner.

Enjoying people-watching as I ate, I felt a sudden drop of air pressure in the room; past experience told me something was manifesting. Setting my plate on my lap, I sat waiting and watching. At first it was a distortion of energy that came through the doorway into the room. As it manifested, I could see a grey, misty figure. I froze, my heart began to race as my breath quickened. "Be Calm, Be Calm," I said to myself as I fought my flight response. Remaining in my seat, trying hard not to react.

People notice when someone is in distress, whether through body language, facial expressions and a few other ways. I didn't want attention brought to me, trying to speak in this state would make matters much worse. I slowly began eating as I tracked the misty figure with my peripheral vision. I needed to keep an eye on it, knowing exactly where it was, gave me a sense of control with an encounter.

Watching as it drifted through the room, I noticed the mist become denser like a shadow. It moved so much slower than the pace of the people in the room, completely out of sync. As it moved passed a few people, it did two stop action movements and began moving as fast as everyone in the room. I couldn't help but notice the different reactions people had. Most people were completely oblivious to the shadow moving past them. There were times when it stopped and stood behind people. When it stopped behind a middle-aged man, the man stopped talking. He turned to the left, then to the right, expecting to see someone. Not seeing anyone standing behind him, he shrugged with a nervous laugh. He didn't realize his instincts were spot on, there was something there.

I continued watching the reactions and non-reactions of the different people. I saw one lady actually do the shivers, spinning around to look behind her. She appeared to be very upset by it. I'm almost positive, by her reaction, she knew something was, indeed, there. When my grandmother would do the spine shiver, she would announce, "Oh! Someone walked over my grave!" I found it a little unsettling everytime she said it.

I glanced over to the other side of the room and noticed a man sitting and enjoying his food. A much older gentleman, he reminded me of Santa Clause, with his white beard and hair. As I became fixated on him I noticed as he continued eating he was watching this shadow. I was surprised, not only did he see it, he was looking straight at it! I felt a sense of relief and even a little excitement. He could see it too! While still fixated on him, the shadow moved out of the room. Suddenly, he turned and looked at me and nodded. Startled, I did a little jump and smiled shyly for staring so long. He nodded again and gently smiled at me, giving me a wink before going back to enjoying his food. He was so calm; the shadow was no big deal to him.

I went back to eating my meal, becoming lost in thought. Dwelling and musing over what just happened. Finally, I came to the conclusion I'd much rather know when something is near me than to be oblivious. Simply because it's there...

"Whether I see it or not."

9. An Orange Inside

I knew a lady, I'll call her Bea, who had recently lost the love of her life. For months, she felt ill but assumed it was due to mourning, which many agreed was probably why. It is true that when our world falls apart, we have physical symptoms caused by our emotions and broken hearts. But after a few months, it was becoming obvious this was something else.

One evening, we were sitting and talking, and I started seeing images of energy around her. This was something new... I'd not experienced this before. It was like seeing energy waves around her moving sluggishly and slowly, with little black blobs floating in the slow currents. I wasn't sure what I was seeing, but it seemed to match her physical and mental state—she looked very unwell.

Concerned, I asked her, "When was the last time you saw your doctor, Bea?"

"I was at his office recently," she said. "He did some tests, but they came back inconclusive. He didn't find anything wrong." As she went into detail about the tests, my mind drifted off. Images began to form in my mind. I could see a dark circle located inside her, beside her hip. It looked to be about the size of an Orange.

Not understanding what I was seeing, I asked, "Does it hurt beside your left hip?"

Bea replied, "During the examination, it was tender when he pushed there, but he couldn't feel anything." We enjoyed the rest of our chat, thou my mind kept wandering back to the odd image.

As I was getting ready to leave, I felt compelled to get her to investigate the tenderness beside her hip?

I said, "Bea, the tenderness in your hip isn't normal. An ultrasound would be a good idea; just to be sure it's not a serious problem." She began to protest. I tried hard to be gentle and told her that being a big girl, sometimes it's harder to feel what's happening inside. She nodded and smiled, I hoped she would follow through with the test.

A week had passed, and I hadn't heard from her. The image of the circle inside her, hung in my mind. I called her but it went to voice mail, I left a quick message, as to how she was doing and give me a call. I waited a few more days, becoming worried she hadn't called me back. Calling her again with no answer, I didn't bother to fill her voice mail and hung up. It had been 3 weeks, and still no word. I began to doubt myself. Did I hurt her feelings? Is she mad at me? Was it because she was moving across the city?

It was mid-morning; I was sitting having tea at the kitchen table. As I stared out the window, Bea came to mind. The phone rang, it was Bea! It was so good to hear her voice...

"Oh Cent, I wanted to get a hold of you sooner," She began. "So much has happened! As you know, I was moving 2 weeks ago and right after the move, I was in a lot more pain than usual. So, I called the doctor and asked for an ultrasound. They found a mass beside my left hip. They booked me for surgery within days." I was so relieved to hear the doctor said she is healing well. She thanked me profusely for urging her to get an ultrasound. The tumour was benign but was growing fast and already the size of...

"An Orange Inside."

10. Sleep Paralysis

For years, I have heard people speak and retell their experiences of Sleep Paralysis. Some talk about being awake and only able to open their eyes yet unable to speak or move. Some say they were completely paralyzed and unable to neither open their eyes nor speak. A few stated, it felt like they were being held down and couldn't breathe due to the weight.

Medical Science tells us it is simply the inability to move through the different stages of sleep. Atonia is just a brief loss of muscle control. Stating it can also cause hypnopompic (waking) or hypnagogic (falling asleep) hallucinations.

Some interrupt a Biblical meaning, insight into spiritual warfare, and demonic attacks. This suggests a need for divine intervention. Brazilian folklore names it as the demon Pisadeira (she who steps), who walks or stands on the chest of people.

Cultures around the world have their own explanations. Some people believe it's Aliens or Sleep Demons attacking when we are vulnerable. Others believe it is Incubus or Succubus that are the cause. Canadian Inuit, may say spells of shamans cause sleep paralysis. The east coast of Canada calls it Old Hag Syndrome, a witch-like creature with evil intent. In Japanese folklore, it is a vengeful spirit that suffocates its enemies in their sleep. Have you ever seen that 1781 painting called "The Nightmare"? It depicts a gremlin crouching on top of a woman. When you stare at this painting, it gets more disturbing.

The more you research, the more you will find on this phenomenon. I believe there is usually a nugget of truth behind belief and folklore. Until you experience it yourself, you can't truly understand this fear. I used to believe medical science answered all causes of sleep paralysis. Still do in most cases, until I started to have escalating issues trying to wake up.

The first time it happened to me, I woke up confused. I was unable to open my eyes and then realized I couldn't move. It was like being trapped inside your body. Logic told me it was just sleep paralysis, but it was still hard to relax and wait it out. I tried wiggling my toes and fingers, not sure if it helped but the paralysis left after a few moments. The experience left me a little unsettled for a few days.

More than a month had passed when it happened again. It had been a busy weekend; spring gardening and clean-up was exhausting. I decided to take a catnap before making dinner. I had just begun to drift off when someone came to my bedroom door. Assuming it was one of the children trying to decide whether to wake me or not, I tried to open my eyes only to realize I was completely paralyzed. Struggling to gain control of my body only made it worse. When I tried to relax I had the sense that someone was standing beside my bed. All of a sudden, I felt a physical weight on my back and started having trouble breathing. In every way, it was absolutely terrifying!

I began screaming in my mind over and over again, "Let me go, let me go!!" It made no difference. Anger began to wash away my fear, and I stopped trying to physically break free. Yelling from within, "Get out, Get out of here! You are not welcome!" There was an immediate release.

Rolling over quickly, I saw movement in the doorway before it moved out of the room. Springing to my feet I ran after it and out the door into the living room, cursing at it and calling out, "Don't Ever Come Back!" My heart was racing as I gasped for breath. It took a few minutes to take back control of my emotions before I could move from that spot.

That was many years ago, and I've not had a problem since. A valuable lesson that day. Listen to your instincts, listen to your inner voice that tells you, you are in danger. There is a difference between fear setting in due to paralysis and fear you are not alone and feel helpless. Fight back spiritually or through shear strength of will. Don't allow fear to consume you, no matter what, because it does little good.

I would like to take this opportunity to say, to all those I have dismissed in the past, I am Truly Sorry. This worldwide phenomenon is frightening and I stoped believing it is always just a simple case of...

"Sleep Paralysis."

11. The Basement

As a young family, we moved around a lot. Each home was a quiet and, for the most part, happy home. At the time, I thought all the things that go Bump in the Night were over. Not realizing it was simply the houses had good happy energy. We had been living in a lovely little house with a large vegetable garden, a row of red currents, an apple tree and two pear trees. Unfortunately, after a few years, the owners decided to tear it down and build a four-plex. Our lease over, we had little choice but to move again.

The house we ended up moving to wasn't a happy house. I hadn't had the chance to see it before we moved in. A toddler and a new baby made it difficult for me to help house hunt. On the day of our move, I entered the house through the front door. It seemed to suit our needs; a 2 bedroom was good since the baby still needed to be in our room. Having two little boys, they could share a bedroom later, since they were large bedrooms.

We had lots of help moving in, the front and back door was a constant flood of our belongings coming in. I decided the 2 children and I would hang in the kitchen since that needed to be my focus to unpack to feed the family. Toddler in his highchair with snacks and a drink, and baby in his wicker bassinette, I started unpacking boxes and organizing the kitchen.

Finally, the last load was being moved in, some destined for the basement. I went to the top of the stairs and asked, "What's down there?" I was told it's just an unfinished basement. Standing at the top of the stairwell, it felt so foreboding, so...dark. It was an open double stair well with no doorframe or door, it left me unsettled. I went back to work in the kitchen and shook it off, after all, the rest of the house seemed nice.

Over the next few weeks, we unpacked and settled in, and routines fell back into place. I was told there were no washer or dryer, not even a hook-up in the basement, so we got a small wash machine that hooked up to the kitchen sink. It was easier than trying to juggle with two little ones at the Laundromat.

Not wanting to go down to the basement every day, I had decided to put the litter for my two cats in the back porch just off the kitchen. For a few weeks, things were fine; though the basement haunted my mind enough that I never went down there. Day by day, the darkness downstairs made me nervous, each time I went to clean the litter in the back porch, I would feel the darkness of the basement and would stare down the stairwell. I had noticed my two cats never went down in the basement either. I was thankful I had no need to go down.

I hated using the back door; it was like the darkness was spreading, moving up out of the basement and into the stairwell. Often times I would step out of the back door, walking backwards to go out and hang the laundry on the clothesline. The feeling of something behind me was becoming difficult to deal with. It got so I used the front door as often as I could. After only 3 weeks, I voiced I couldn't live here anymore, we needed to move.

One afternoon when I went to clean the cat litter in the back porch, I felt a wave of heavy energy coming from the basement. Standing up, I went to the top of the stairs and stared down into the stairwell. I felt a heaviness begin to envelop me and a slight dizziness. There was a pulling effect, a feeling of being pulled down into the basement. Like a special effect in a movie, the bottom of the stairs suddenly zoomed up to me, overwhelming me. Gasping, I stumbled backward, catching my balance against the wall. The air pressure became dense and a wall of darkness pushed me against the wall. I struggled to breath, paralyzed with fear. I could hear someone screaming... it was me!

In the distance, I could hear my little boy yelling, "Mommy, Mommy!" The baby was crying in the background. My children were frightened as was I. The urgency to help them gave me the strength within to fight back. I composed myself and brought forth the primitive fearlessness and aggression we all have within us, desperation and the wrath of a mother bear erupted.

In a voice I didn't recognize, I growled at it, "Let go of me!" I shoved my hands forward, pushing it back with all my might, and ran out of the porch.

Picking my little boy up off his play mat in the living room, I walked backward into my bedroom and closed the door. Rubbing his back, I kissed his cheek and told him everything is okay. Grabbing some toys from the crib, I handed them to my toddler as I sat him down and picked up the baby. Within a few minutes, the baby started to settle down, so I sat down in my rocking chair.

"Would you like Mama to tell you a story?" My toddler grinned and climbed up onto my lap. I slowly rocked with my two little boys cuddled in my arms, "Once upon a time, there was a beautiful garden full of flowers and butterflies...." Slowly each child fell asleep before I had finished my story. I continued to slowly rock back and forth as I delved deep into contemplation. I started to feel calm and safe with my two little boys nestled in my arms. Dinner is going to be a little late tonight.

The darkness was no longer just in the basement. It enshrouded the stairs and porch now. I tried to see what it was but it was like a thick fog I couldn't see through. It became difficult to work in the kitchen; I was so grateful to move shortly after. We only lived in that little house for two months, now I knew why it was cheap and hard to rent out.

Whatever it was, that came upstairs and into the porch was now out of...

"The Basement."

12. This Old Century House

We had been living in a nice newer home, but it was too long of a drive for work, and we found ourselves house-hunting yet again. I started having daydreams about a house, a large red-brick older home on a corner lot with a grand entrance. Something seemed very odd about the house. It appeared to have no front walk leading to the road, and something seemed wrong with the address.

About a week later, we drove into the small city closer to work, to view an available house. It was on a corner lot and the driveway was at the side of the house. I voiced the house felt familiar. It was a large pale yellow brick house, well maintained, with numbers above the side door. How strange, I thought perhaps the house was divided into 2 apartments. We walked up the pathway along the side of the house to the front door, where we were to meet.

A weird sensation started spreading through me, a warping feeling as I slowed my walk to a snail's pace. Through my eyes, it was like looking down a desert road as the heat rose in hazy waves. Realizing I was walking through a déjà vu, it dawned on me why the house felt familiar. I voiced, "This is the house of my daydream, we will be living here." I was quickly shushed in case the owners could hear me. Sometimes, I would forget myself and blurt things out. I mean...who would rent to a crazy sounding person, right?

The Front steps sat on a large cement platform. There was no walkway that led to the road in front of the house. It made sense since there was no sidewalk at the bottom of the steep hill. It would have led out to the curb of a busy road. I also noticed the front door had no house number. *Something wrong with the address* in my daydream was now answered. The house's address was the side of the house not the front. Knocking on the door I noticed beside the stairs red brick was peeking out the side, someone had painted over the brick. I thought to myself, what a shame.

Stepping into the house, it was beautiful, with a large front foyer. All the rooms were large, living and dining rooms on the left and a great big kitchen on the right. A large bathroom with a tub had 2 doors, one for the kitchen and one for the hall at the back. There was a wide room at the back divided from the main house with a heavy wood door. It was perfect for running a part-time business out of. Upstairs were 3 large bedrooms and a small bathroom with a shower, it too had two doors, one for the hallway and one for the master bedroom.

I could already see us living there and was excited! However, there was a space on the second floor that felt heavy. It was above the front foyer, which mirrored the size of the downstairs. Figured some plants and lace curtains might brighten up the gloom. With no basement, I could see nothing but the plus side to living here.

For the most part things were going great, my 2 little boys settled in quickly and we started to enjoy living in such a big house. Within a few months, uneasiness settled in; something on the second floor seemed... off. The peace and quiet of this house didn't last long. Arguments were numerous and became the norm. Communication stopped and we lived in silence. Learning I was pregnant, we sat down and had a heart-to-heart talk, deciding to try and make it work. My baby girl was born 7 months later. She was a quiet baby, easy to sooth and care for. This was a blessing with 5 and 3-year-old little boys running around. I had little time for anything other than being a mother.

Soon after, my black Persian cat Bear suddenly became very ill and I rushed him to the emergency vet, he died on the table. The vet felt something ruptured inside, as his belly was like jello. I had no proof but I've a theory what happened to him. My other cat, Ally started to have seizures, falling and getting hurt. The vet felt it was best to put him down, since he was an elderly cat in pain and was traumatized by the seizures.

A few nights after Ally cat was euthanized, I had just finished the late-night feeding for the baby. Turning off the lamp and crawling into bed, I stared at the moon shining in the window. Settling in and closing my eyes, I felt a cat jump up at the foot of my bed and walk up the side and onto my pillow. It was familiar and at first, I didn't think much about it until remembering... I no longer had any cats. Popping my eyes open, right beside my face was the head of a cat! I panicked and pulled away quickly in shock and surprise!

It flew past me to the opposite wall and up to the ceiling above the crib. Was it a bat!? Quickly, I got out of bed and turned on the lamp, there was nothing there. Thinking if it was a bat, it could have fallen down into the crib!? Running over I found the baby was sleeping peacefully, I checked her blankets and along the bumper pad, nothing. Checking between the wall and crib, I got down on my hands and knees, looking under. I looked everywhere and still, found nothing. I sat on the floor in the moonlight for a long time, trying to make sense of it and assure myself the baby is safe.

Finally getting up and running my fingers through my hair, as I slowly walked back to bed. I sat on the side of the bed and stared out the window at the moon. What is it about this house? What's going on in...

"This Old Century House?"

13. The Man Upstairs

This story took place in The Old Century House but warrants its own tale to tell. It occurred just before my daughter was born when I was 30 years old. I began to write about these strange occurrences. Not wanting to reveal the story was about me, I often wrote in the 3rd person. For most people in my life I kept these occurrences secret, my skeleton in the closet.

This next story is directly out of my journal as is. It was a turning point in my life of understanding and learning to stand my ground.

Truth or Fiction, a Ghost story. By Cent 1991.

The sun was bright and the birds welcomed in the day. It was a beautiful morning, but something just didn't feel right, like getting up on the wrong side of the bed. The breakfast dishes done, and her two little boys playing quietly, now would be a good time to catch up on the ironing.

While the pile of ironing went down, the young mother had an ever-growing sense she was not alone. Frowning, she tried hard to ignore it, until suddenly, she felt someone was watching her. She spun around quickly, thinking someone was looking at her through the window. Only to feel foolish and embarrassed, realizing she was on the second floor.

Quickly, she packed up the ironing and hurried down the stairs. A picture kept flashing through her mind of an older man in a beige trench coat wearing a gentleman's hat.

Within minutes the children came clambering down the stairs. "Can we play in the living room mommy," the eldest asks.

"Yes, but why not play upstairs with your toys, rather than down here?" Mother questioned.

"We got scared and decided to come downstairs," he replied.

The little one still in diapers, pout's and demands to be picked up. As she bends down, he wraps his arm's tightly around her neck and buries his head. "What's the matter honey?" she gently prods.

"Man in da hall scare me," replied the toddler.

Her knees grow weak. She takes a deep breath, "What man?"

"Man in da coat and da hat," he replied.

As evening fell, it seemed harder than usual to settle the children down to bed. It had been an exhausting day and she decided to retire early. After checking one more time on the little ones she walks down the hall to her room. Sensing something, she stops. She can't help staring at the corner in the hall. Standing there for a long moment, the sound of her husband's heavy footsteps coming up the stairs brings her back.

"What was that!?" Her eyes popped open to the blackness. She listened in the night. One of the children is whimpering. With urgency, she goes to see to her child. Turning on the little lamp in his bedroom, she's confused by the haze and rubs her eyes.

He laid there in a little ball, whimpering as he slept. It feels cold. She reaches out to rub his arm. It was like ice. Fear crept over her, instinctively, she climbs into his bed, wrapping her arms around him and drawing him close. "Mommy, make him go away," he whispers. A shiver runs through her spine.

She kisses him and whispers, "I'm right here."

By the next day, the children refused to go upstairs. The feeling of anger was beginning to wash away her fear. It fed her courage. She stomped up the stairs and down the hall. "Stop scaring my children, this is my house, and you don't belong here, leave!" she demanded. She waited for a long moment. The feeling of sadness and a sense of loss washed over her. Tears welled up in her eyes. "I'm sorry, but this isn't where you're supposed to be; you have to go now. Follow the light, it has the answers," she said out loud.

The day quickly went by without a hitch. All seemed quiet. As they ate dinner at the dining room table, "So are you kids still scared to go upstairs?" Father asks.

"Nope, Mommy took care of it," answers the eldest.

The children grinning, looking to Mom… "Eat your veggies," she replies.

The problem was over. Understanding came; I didn't have to be scared anymore. No more running, stand my ground. I felt Very protective of my children concerning this stuff. It fed my courage. I don't know who he was but it was the last time I saw…

"The Man Upstairs"

14. Temporary Lodging

Just when life seems easier for a few years, a wrench gets thrown in to trip you up. The landlord was taking possession of the Old Century House and was moving in; we had 30 days. The lease long ago expired changing the rental to a month to month, we had to move. With a 6-year-old, a 4-year-old and a 1-year-old this was going to be tough. Two weeks into packing I was already exhausted and we still hadn't found a new rental. By the third week I was told we would be staying at some guy's student housing rental for a month. Being summertime, the students went home, and 2 bedrooms on the 3rd floor were available, plus the main level bathroom, living room and kitchen. We were allowed to move in immediately, a week to move in was helpful... somewhat.

It was a townhouse; walking through the front door I said, "What kind of fresh hell is this!" I was met with a row of padlocked doors. The hall, living room and kitchen floors were filthy, the bathroom needed scrubbed. Even after I swept and washed the floors, my kids were going to have to play on blankets. I climbed the 2 staircases to the 3rd floor, baby on hip and little guys ahead of me. Doing the best I could to clean, we put the 2 beds and crib, in the one room. There was no room in the tiny room across the hall for anything but our bed. We will be living out of boxes and luggage for a month, furniture and boxes piled on the main level.

I was nearing my limit, exhaustion and stress taking its toll. Yet, the first night in that tiny bedroom, I couldn't sleep; there was darkness around the closet bureau. I felt the need to check on the children a number of times, throughout the night. As the weeks went by I tried hard to smile and be happy around my children. I was thankful a school was just down the street. We'd pack a lunch and snacks, plenty of water and juice. Baby's bag was stocked, we spent hours each day at the playground.

3 weeks in, I started seeing a shadow move from the hall to the closet bureau in my room. I told myself, "Just one more week and we're moving, stay calm." I gotta tell you... the creep factor was at a high level; worry for my children and knowing while I'm sleeping, this shadow could have walked into the room. I tried to act like I was oblivious to its existence. My hope was to just blend in with the norm of people coming and going in this usually busy student housing.

The last night before our move, I noticed the heaviness; the darkness by the closet bureau was gone. Did ignoring its existence work? I had sure hoped so, but we were moving tomorrow so it no longer mattered. While the children slept on the 3rd floor, I was busy packing the last of the kitchen. After organizing for breakfast in the morning, it was time for bed. Tomorrow is a big day and it was late. I still had the last of the bedrooms to pack in the morning and ensure the diaper bag was stocked, but it could wait.

I was tired of the constant moving around, so over it. With 2 little boys and a baby, I felt I couldn't do it anymore. Trudging up the 2 flights of stairs for the umpteenth time that day, I checked on the children then slipped into bed. Sleep came quickly but late into the night I was woke by the sound of the baby moving around in her crib fussing. As I entered the room, the streetlight outside the window provided enough light without turning on the lamp. There was a dark dense shadow beside the crib. Alarmed I move forward and the shadow moved away and into the corner of the room. Rubbing her back and nestling her in I whispered, "You're okay Baby, Mommy's here."

My youngest little boy started murmuring in his sleep, tossing in his bed. "Please leave us alone, go away," I whispered. The darkness moved farther into the corner where I couldn't see it but everything within me told me it was still there. There was no way I was leaving the room and decided that I was sleeping in the kid's room for the rest of the night. Crawling into bed with him and stroking his hair, I tucked up the blankets. It was a very low little youth bed, thou wide enough for the 2 of us; the soles of my feet were up against the footboard, giving my head just a teeny space to spare. I laid there with my eyes closed, fighting my fear.

Wham! The footboard slammed hard against my feet, causing the bed to jerk. Panic-stricken, I yanked my feet up and rolled into a ball. A second shove came right after, and my little boy tried to bury himself under me. He was shaking like a leaf, I wrapped my arms around him and said, "I'm here, you're safe, Mommy has you!" Pulling the blanket up and around us, I squeezed my eyes shut unwilling to look to the foot of the bed. I felt paralyzed with fear, remaining frozen, not daring to move. Only a couple of hours and the sun will be up. Time to get the hell out of Dodge and away from this...

"Temporary Lodging"

15. The Adult Education Centre

We had moved to a village just outside the small city. The house was a little run down but cheap and convenient and best of all it was what I called a quiet house. We lived there for a number of years; the 2 schools in the village were great. One school was for JK to grade 4 and the other school grades 5 thru 8. A lot of kids were bussed in from the surrounding area. It wasn't long before all three children were in school, time sure can fly.

Being a High School dropout, I decided it was time to get my grade 12 diploma. When I was a young student, my average grade was a C and I also did poorly in high school. After an operation on my throat, I was unwell for almost a month. I missed so much school and was so far behind I gave up, dropped out and got a job. I now planned on changing that failure and registered at an adult education centre in the city. A grade 12 diploma was a step towards higher education.

Finally, it was orientation day; I was a little early, so I sat in the car in the parking lot. There was a row of old buildings, with courtyards to each side, trees and plants overgrown. The buildings were actually impressive; at the time, I wasn't sure what they were once used for. Scanning the 2rd floor while I waited, there was a woman standing in front of a window in the north wing of the education centre.

I had preregistered, choosing classes I needed and some easy ones like typing for easy credits. Schedule in hand I found my seat, it was explained we are allowed to use calculators for math. We never were allowed calculators when I was a student. Math and history were my worse subjects. At the end of the orientation, we were told parts of the building including the wings, were off limits with stairwells and hallways locked. So... who was the woman on the second floor I saw in the window??

Driving home to my village, the image of the woman on the second floor, kept coming to mind. Come to think of it, something seemed off about her. She just stood there staring down at the overgrown courtyard. It was creepy; a shiver ran up my spine.

I decided to do some research on the history of these buildings. The 3 identical buildings were dated 1840. One building was for the disabled, one was for the mentally insane and the other was to house the criminally insane. It was labeled an Insane Asylum, I was somewhat thankful the education centre, was for the mentally insane building and not for the criminally insane.

Around the mid 1900's, these people were considered patients, and the terms mentally and physically disabled were used. New accommodations and caregivers were set up, and they closed those two buildings. A few years later, the patients labeled criminally insane were moved to a facility in a different city. The buildings were then used as homes for the aged. The woman I saw in the upstairs window was young... the question is, was she dead or alive?

In the 1990's, the buildings were deemed unsuitable for residency, and they closed off 2 of the buildings, leaving one available for the Adult Education Centre. I took solace in the fact; that the problem wasn't at my house to deal with. I was only going to be there for the winter and then I'll have my grade 12 diploma.

Over the next 2 months, I only saw the woman in the window once more. Couldn't help but overhear people talking about the building being haunted. One day in typing class a lady I befriended named Janet leaned over to me and quietly said to me, "Did you hear about the weird stuff going on upstairs?"

"No I haven't. What kind of weird stuff?" I whispered back.

Janet's voice was hushed but filled with excitement, "Up in the old cafeteria, there's a spot that is crazy weird. Come upstairs with me at lunch break and I'll show you!" Curious, I agreed. One of the staircases was accessible; the other one near the wing of the building was locked. The second floor was open and empty, what was once the old cafeteria was at the end of the hall. As we approached, we could see three much younger women darting back and forth in a small area. Their nervous giggling told the story.

Stopping and turning to Janet, "Let me guess," I said sarcastically, "That's the weird area," Grinning she nods. When the 3 ladies left, we walked into the cafeteria. Janet walked through first, turning around she stared at me, her eyes big, hands folded under her chin.

"Your turn," she said in a nervous voice. Slowly, I stepped forward; the air pressure began to change. With each step, it became denser and heavier. Breathing became difficult, quickening my pace I hurried out of the area. We walked out into the hall and over to a window facing the parking lot; I could see the wing of the building and had a bird's eye view of the courtyard. We agreed the dense energy felt heavy and concentrated in the old cafeteria. Not sure the cause and to be frank, I didn't want to know.

Staring down into the courtyard, I caught movement in a window on the second floor of the wing. It was that odd woman I had seen twice before. To my horror, she jumped through the glass window, falling down into the courtyard. Her body laid there broken, slowly she became misty. She got up and walked out of the courtyard and into the overgrown brush, fading as she left.

"Tell me what you saw," Janet's voice startled me. "I know you saw her; I've seen her standing looking out the window as well."

I explained, "Actually, this is the 3rd time I've seen her but this time she jumped out the window to her death." She was quiet for a moment and explained to me, some call it a death loop. Although she felt this wasn't a spirit trapped in her last minutes on earth. To her it was just a ghost. It was a loop in time, a fragmented piece of energy repeating itself.

I never went back upstairs again, neither did Janet. It was nice to have someone to talk to about weird stuff. She blurted out a warning to me, "Don't go down and around the corner to the locked doors of the wing. There is a man standing on the other side of the glass door. He is as he was in life." That didn't sound good to me, I took her advice.

Just before graduation, we came across the principal and a few students talking about seeing someone in the upstairs window of the wing. The principal said maintenance had heard noises up there and felt it was probably a vagrant.

I voiced, "Dust the floors with flour so you can see where they are getting in and where they have been." The Principal thought it was a good idea. Walking away, I said, "Of course, if no footprints are found, it's something else here in..."

"The Adult Education Centre."

16. Warp Your Noodle

I started paying attention to what I had been calling daydreams. I noticed they would manifest at a later date. I began to journal the events and discovered it took 3-5 days, sometimes 7-10 days to manifest. There were times I'd see a mini-movie right before it happened or an image of someone, and they'd show up or call me on the phone. I even logged the duration of the mini-movies, some seconds like a flash, some minutes worth of moving images; I was trying to make sense of it all.

What really didn't make sense were the ones that seemed to have no meaning. For instance, a mini-movie showed me in the city to the west of us and I saw my eldest son's old friend and his mom. It had been years since they had moved out of the village. Seeing each other kitty-corner at a main crossroad, she waves, I wave back. Crossing we met up, it seemed like idle chit-chat and nothing more. We departed, going our separate ways.

This mini-movie played out 8 days later, exactly the same. I had expected our conversation was important but... it was just a catch-up chat. We parted ways, never seeing her again. So I'd ask myself, what is the point? I mean why see it to begin with, if there is nothing important or meaningful?

For the most part I was careful of what I said and how I said it. Choosing my words carefully so as not to be discovered or thought of as being creepy, the skeleton in my closet. Often I felt torn between being discovered and guilt for not voicing a warning. Even small events some people would notice and I would quickly explain it away. I remember one afternoon during a get-together at the lake; I was sitting at the kitchen table and saw in my mind a tea cup slide off the table beside me. Sure enough, someone set a teacup down not far from where I was sitting. So I waited, and someone else came along, setting a large platter on the table. She pushed the platter across the table and the teacup was on the move, sliding off the table. My hand went out faster than my head turned to look. I caught it mid-air by the saucer, not a drop of tea was spillt. There was an awkward silence in the kitchen as everyone turned and stared at me. I voiced, "Wow, I can't believe I caught that. I saw it move out of the corner of my eye!" I mean… it wasn't a lie; I was keeping an eye on it.

My youngest sister chirped in, "WOW, you have fast reflexes!" Others chuckled in agreement. As she left the room she stopped in the doorway, she turned to me and gave me a knowing grin. Her body moved in a chuckle as she turned and walked away. I thanked her later for the backup. You see when you know something is going to happen before it happens and it becomes habitual, some people get very uncomfortable or creeped out when it happens to often. She was not one of them.

I had lost a 5-year friendship because I became too at ease blurting things out rather than choosing my words wisely. There is a fine line to something being creepy to you being creepy. Our friendship drifted apart, ending in a handful of phone calls. It made her to uncomfortable for her to continue a friendship. Lesson learned. Be careful and thoughtful how others react, and act accordingly.

A funny scenario played out during a Canada Day celebration up at the lake. Most of the family and even some close friends enjoyed the warm summer day. Little kids playing in the sand and shallows, teens enjoying swimming and water toys. Dad was manning the grill while some of the other men gathered around the BBQ ... as men do. Mom called out, "Can someone get the Juice out of the fridge and bring the tray of cups out to the beach?"

I started to head to the door when one of my nieces called out, "I'll get them, Grandma!" I took the opportunity to have a sit down in a lawn chair beside my youngest sister for a wee chit-chat. A mini-movie manifested almost immediately. It showed my niece walking towards the beach carrying a large tray. There is an old driftwood tree lying between the grass and beach; we often sit on it. I saw her misjudge where it was and tripped over it, skinning her shins and dropping the tray. Watching the corner of the cottage as we chit-chatted, I waited for her to appear. She was almost to the beach and off the path.

I called out to her, "Be careful, don't trip over the log!" She checked ahead of her and changed her direction, thanking me.

My sister leaned close, "You saw that before it happened didn't you?"

I whispered, "Yes but ask yourself, would it have happened whether I mentioned it or not?" She stared at me with a frown. I continued, "Don't think too hard on that, it can..."

"Warp Your Noodle."

17. Those Bearing Gifts

Sometimes, things are barely seen, like it's sitting in your blind spot, and each time you turn to look it moves, staying within that blind spot. My creep factor is stronger when I can't see it. I find it unnerving when something is trying to stay hidden.

At first it was just a flash of darkness I would catch from the corner of my eye. Standing farther back than my peripheral vision could see. I decided to ignore it with two different theories in mind. Either it will resolve itself and end, or it will get bolder and let its guard down. After more than a week, it was becoming more obvious and slower at reacting to my turning around. It was getting far too close for my comfort, maybe 6' away. I had enough and spoke, "I know you are there, I can see you." Immediately, it pulled away and disappeared. Of course… it didn't end there, hence this story.

Things were quiet for a few weeks, no slivers of darkness just out of sight. Until, one evening I was sitting in the living room painting a miniature house for a Christmas village and saw a sliver on my left at the 10 o'clock position. The sliver started to distort as a wavy type energy began to manifest. Slowly, it started to transform, taking shape. It looked like a small misty blob about 3 feet high.

I tried hard to steady my nerves and pretend I didn't notice it. My hands to shaky to paint, I began cleaning my brushes instead. An image came to my mind of a small, sad little boy. *Not sure where the image came from.* A small boy slowly started to manifest; he looked just like the picture in my mind. I felt somewhat sad, thinking perhaps he is lost and confused. He just stood in the dining room and stared at me. Gradually, he began to dissolve as he walked away, disappearing.

One day, In the middle of the afternoon, a mentor/friend and I were enjoying a chit-chat in my living room, about this event of a small boy. Twenty minutes passed when I began feeling something was manifesting, I could see a distortion not far from me. My friend asked me, "What are you seeing?"

"I think he is here," I answered. She nods knowingly as he continued to manifest.

"Describe what you see and feel Cent," was her reply.

I began, "It's a sad little boy, maybe 6 or 7 years old. His clothes are old and soiled, his hair is messy and he is in need of a bath. I feel an overwhelming sadness from him." As I was describing what I was seeing, the boy began to change, and seemed lighter, brighter. From behind his back, he pulled out a bouquet of flowers. "How strange he is giving me flowers I can see the colour of the flowers so vividly. I don't ever remember seeing colour like that, it's never happened before," I told her. With a shy smile the little boy gestured that the flowers were for me. I couldn't help but notice one flower was misplaced about to fall out of the bouquet.

In the distance, I could hear my friend say, "Cent…something doesn't feel right." It felt like I was being drawn in, a sense of detachment washed over me as I leaned towards him. I had an overwhelming urge to reach out and fix the flower. The little boy urged with a desperate smile, yes…yes touch the flower.

"CENT!!!" she yelled. With that, his face began to contort into an evil sideways grin. Shocked, I jumped back in a startled reflex as the boy spun on his heels and disappeared.

"Holy Crap, what was that!?" I exclaimed.

"It was a Trickster!" she said. "Tell me, what was the bait it used to lure you?"

I sat for a minute, mulling it over in my mind. It dawned on me; the trickster was using my weaknesses against me. Finally, I said, "It used my heart for children in distress, my love of flowers, and my issue with things needing to be straightened and in order."

"You're exactly right!" She exclaimed. "It has no doubt been watching you, found your weaknesses, and used them to trick you. It was masking itself as a child to deceive you, using the out of place flower to make you reach out to it."

I broke out in goose bumps, feeling venerable and betrayed. "What can I do to prevent being tricked like that again?" I asked her, hoping her answer would make me feel safe.

"Your eyes can deceive you," she said. "You can't just rely on what you can see. You must learn to use your other senses. Feel the energy in the room, the lower vibration is very different than ours and that which is higher. Trust your instincts they won't let you down." She leaned back in her chair and was silent for a moment. She chuckled, "Most of all, beware of..."

"Those Bearing Gifts."

18. A Home of Our Own

Finally, the opportunity came to buy a house, a rent to own. It was situated just outside of the village up on the hill. It even had a bit of acreage, which would be great. We were told it was available on January 1st, and everyone was excited, especially the boys. Having four bedrooms, they would finally have their very own rooms!

I decided the two bedrooms' upstairs were for the boys. My daughter could have the one at the foot of the stairs. The last room was on the other side of the house. I was a little nervous at first about being that far away from the kid's rooms at night. They seemed fine with it, so... all was good. We made the deal and signed on the dotted line.

It was a surprise when we were contacted less than a week later and told we could move in anytime at no extra cost. The tenants were moving out early and the owner thought it would be wonderful for us to spend Christmas in our new home. "The first month is free!" he said. I laughed and thanked him for his thoughtfulness.

After a family discussion, it was decided we'd hold off getting the Christmas Tree and move in 2 weeks before Christmas Day. All the children were so excited they were asking for boxes to start packing their rooms. It was gonna be a lot of work but I was confident it was doable.

Moving day arrived! With lots of help from family and friends, things moved smoothly. Boxes all marked ended up in the right rooms. Christmas boxes were designated for the living room; we were moved in within no time. While beds were being put together and the kids were organizing their new rooms, I concentrated on the kitchen. I needed to make sandwiches; it was time for a break. We gathered around the dining room table for a late lunch when my youngest asked, "What's that on the wall?" I looked over and saw the stain of a dripping cross.

"Some people bless a house when they move in honey," I replied. Changing the subject, I added, "We should go get our Christmas tree tomorrow!" Everyone nodded in agreement.

There were a few items in the garage the old tenant still needed to pick-up. I met him downstairs in the garage. The guy was friendly enough but he was acting oddly, like he desperately wanted to tell me something yet unable to find the words. "Well... good luck in your new home," he said.

He handed me his set of keys to the garage but when I tried to take them he gripped them tighter, unwilling to let them go. Looking up at his face our eyes locked, his face looked troubled. In a quiet voice he said, "Be safe..." his voice trailing off. Releasing the keys, he walked away, looking back at me before getting in his truck. I recognized that look, my heart sank. I thought of the cross stain on the dining room wall. Was he trying to warn me? Was something going on in the house?

Christmas was wonderful, and the children quickly settled into their new bedrooms. All was well. January was filled with unpacking, organizing, and decorating the house. It finally felt like home as we all fell easily into our routines... we were happy. Come early February, I started noticing the dining room and back hall had an odd feeling. Feeling like the air pressure change when a thunderstorm was blowing in.

I was in the kitchen baking, when my eldest son came into the room. He stood there for a moment, just staring wide-eyed at me. "What's wrong?" I asked.

"We don't like hanging out in brothers' room... something's wrong, it feels creepy," he said.

I headed for the stairs with son in tow. "I best have a look see," I told him. As I reached the upstairs landing, the air pressure began to drop. It felt incredibly strong walking through the door into the bedroom. Turning to my son I said, "Ya, it's very heavy in here, isn't it? Let's crack the window open a bit and burn a sage stick to take care of it." They nodded and went and played Nintendo.

The next day I noticed a specific area in the dining room had that same heavy feel to it when you walked through it. Walking through it a few times I determined it was about a 4' circle. Decided to cleanse the house and get my sage bundle out to do the whole house. I left the sage bundle in the basement by the furnace to smolder... just for good measure. It would allow the furnace to blow the smoke through the house. Foolish of me not to have cleansed the house sooner, I know better. My excuse, we moved so fast, and things have been busy... a lame excuse, I know.

After a few weeks, the house felt much lighter. That whole year passed without incident. Things went smoothly as we moved through life. We made plans and started the vegetable garden and flowerbeds, enjoying our 2nd Christmas in our new house.

I was sipping a tea when I looked up and saw my son standing there with that wide-eyed stare… "Mom, it's starting again!" he said. The sound of alarm carried in his voice.

"What do you mean? What's starting again?" I asked.

He frowned at me and said, "That weird creepy feeling upstairs, just like last February!" Come to think of it, he was right. It was also in February of last year, the house had that heavy feel to it. Why the heck was it happening again? What does it mean? Is it a coincidence?

"Okay honey, thanks for letting me know. I'll take care of it," I said trying to sound confident. So…I saged the house again, since it worked last time. I also started adding salt to the bucket when I washed the floors. It did seem to dissipate it some in the dining room and upstairs but it lingered for a while and then it was gone.

Dam it… what the hell is going on!? A year had passed, this will be the 3rd February in a row. It was suggested to me to open a bible in the bedroom upstairs which seemed to help. Thou the dining room increased in energy. Did I divert it, concentrating it in the dining room? Something was active in the 4' circle that has been a problem in the past. It's time to stay alert watch the dining room closely.

Sure enough, I started seeing shadows move through that area. They always moved in the same direction, from the east to the west towards the kitchen. Within a few weeks, the circle became very dense and pressurized, enough to make me step around it rather than walk through it.

By the middle of February, there was definitely a presence in the dining room and not just in the circle area. Something was now moving around in the dining room and hall that led upstairs. Along one wall, there were three arches from the kitchen into the rest of the house. Many times it felt like something was watching me through the middle arch while I was in the kitchen. It was unsettling and I starting to feel ticked off about it. I decided the next time I see something moving through the circle... I would head it off and confront it. Boy that a mistake!

I had been washing dishes and cleaning the fridge out when I saw something move through the dining room circle. I slammed the fridge door shut and ran to the centre archway. Something big was standing there! It was like a wall of energy between us but it came crashing through at me, I was horrified! My twin brother's image flashed beside me. I stumbled backwards and continued walking backward as it shoved its way into the kitchen! I backed up until I reached the sink; it was there that I stood my ground.

It came right up to me, about a foot away, menacing and threatening it stood there looming over me. I was absolutely terrified to the point I felt cut in half. From the waist up, I felt dizzy and floating. From the waist down was heavy and felt detached, and yet I could see my lower half in tremors. It stood there for what felt like ages as I coward.

Finally, I shoved both my hands into the dishwater and closed my eyes, unwilling to look at it. Blocking what was all around me to become self-contained. My own little safety bubble, to feel whole again and stop the tremors still coursing through my feet and legs. Within a few minutes, it dissipated and left.

Like I said, boy was that a mistake... I just opened a can of worms. There was never any activity in the kitchen before but it was obvious whatever it was, it was no longer contained in the dining room. I knew that I needed to face my fear and deal with this again next February. I will not allow anyone, including myself to be bullied, harassed, or threatened. There will be no running; it has been to many years of waiting to finally have...

"A Home of Our Own."

19. The February Man

I began a new journal, remembering events logging every little detail I could. Knowing I had almost a year before February rolled around to prepare myself. In the beginning, it was only about a week or two at the start of the month but after 3 years it was now the whole month that the house became active.

Logic was telling me that this wasn't simply what I refer to as a ghost. To me a ghost is more a fragment of energy in time that repeats itself. It's not aware of anything past the loop. We've all heard of the old woman walking down the hall and disappearing into a room. It's an event that happens over and over again, never deviating. What I was experiencing was interactive, and was fully aware of its actions and of me.

Looking past the fear and the emotional confusion I went through, I had to ask myself, was my reaction the fear of the unknown? The shock of what happened? It didn't really feel like an entity or something evil. I sensed anger and upset yes, but also a sense of something worldly about this energy.

Over the next few months, during quiet times, when I was painting miniatures or sewing, I started having an image of an older man flash in my mind. Come the autumn, two short mini-movies began to replay over and over. One was inside my house but not my belongings and the other showed an old man driving a red tractor up near the pond behind the house. When I was home alone, I started asking out loud, "Who are you? What is your name?" Within two weeks the answers I was seeking came to me in an odd kind of way.

I was at work selling computers in a different county then I lived. A senior couple came up to my glass counter, and we exchanged pleasantries. They casually mentioned they were going up to visit friends in the village. I asked which village, surprised I said, "I live there!" They asked if I knew their friends. I didn't. They went on to tell of another couple they used to know. They had lived up on the hill just outside the village, but the husband past away and the house was sold. I thought to myself... this can't be a coincidence. I prodded for more information.

"You know, I live on the hill, it wouldn't happen to be the white house with green doors and black trim would it?" I questioned. They were excited and enthusiastically offered the story of the people that use to live there some years ago.

"It's a sad story," the old woman explained. She gave the couples names and mentioned they had two daughters. "One morning he woke up confused and didn't recognize his wife and daughters. By the time the ambulance arrived he had passed away. Apparently, he died of a brain aneurysm." The couple shook their heads at the memory.

"That truly is a sad story... So whatever happened to his wife and children?" I asked. They sold the house and they moved to the city I was told. I nodded and added, "Did he use to have an old red tractor?"

"His tractor?" the old woman said. "Why do you ask?"

"I heard a rumour is all, something about his tractor up at the pond," I replied.

The old man started to laugh, he turned to his wife and said, "Remember one winter he misjudged where the pond was and the tractor cracked the ice and fell through!" I chuckled along at the notion.

"Well... I must get back to work," I told them. "Thank-you for stopping in and sharing your stories. Enjoy your visit with friends." They smiled, nodding saying their goodbyes. It was indeed odd they stopped to talk and not once asked about computers. So, what made them stop to talk to me? It certainly wasn't a coincidence that they were the very people that had the answers I was looking for.

That evening I was sewing a button on a shirt, and a thought struck me. A memory from 3 years ago, I had found a small wooden sign in the over-grown thorny bush at the end of the driveway. It read the same name the old couple told of. I went to the garage to see if it was still up on the shelf I had put it on. No such luck, someone must have thrown it out. No matter, I now had a better understanding of what was truly happening in the house. This wasn't some menacing, belligerent spirit trying to bully and harass us. It was a human spirit in a state of confusion. Who the hell were we? Where is his family!?

After Christmas I decided to gather the children together and have a discussion. I explained that the activity in February was of a man who lived here years ago. Little did I know at the time how many years he would be part of our lives, but those are future stories to be told.

We sat there in silence for a few minutes until suddenly...

"So wait...," one child said. "A ghost man appearing every February?" The children all looked at one another and agreed that henceforth, he would be known as...

"The February Man."

20. Their Missing Boy

Aside from the activity that happens in February, we lived our lives enjoying the freedom of owning our own home. My vegetable garden was well established and producing well, the flowers bloomed, and the backyard was alive with insects creating its own eco-system. It was a lot of work processing the harvest.

This story took place one late spring afternoon. I enjoyed cooking and baking, so I was often in the kitchen. Having a large vegetable garden and three children, I was in there even more. To keep me company, I had a radio on top of the fridge and a small portable TV on a side table. I was busy preparing dinner when the 6 o'clock news came on the television. There was an alert of a missing child from a city I knew, just northwest of us.

I went over to the TV and turned up the sound. They were showing a picture of a young boy; I think they said he was 12 years old. When they enlarged the picture to full screen, I was staring at his eyes and I started to see a map in my mind, the northeast of the city highlighted. The news said his parents took away his gaming so he ran away. His bike with his backpack were also gone.

After missing for more than a week, the news was reporting theories and hearsay concerning his whereabouts. Even suggested that maybe he met someone online and may no longer be in the city. I knew that was wrong... the map in my mind, kept showing me the northeast part of the city. I just knew he had to be in that area. I went online to look at a map; it showed the northeast was still a rural area.

Disturbing images started to manifest. I was looking down at a large leafless tree, hovering above and moving in a half circle around the tree top. The grasses were brown and withered and there was an old wire fence running along the bottom of the image. I could see a boy lying at the base of the tree, in a position that was unnatural. There was no bike or backpack in the image that I could see. All summer, the image replayed over and over, haunting my mind. Each time, I contemplated what to do.

There was a hotline... but what would I say? Doubtful they would take me seriously and think I'm off my rocker. Worse case they may launch an investigation against me, thinking I'm somehow involved with his disappearance. Manpower and valuable resources would be wasted on a dead end.

When September rolled around, I was considering driving the hour or more to their city with hopes, perhaps somehow, knowing more of where he is. It was a large rural area... I had no idea where to start. Feelings of frustration and the inability to stop the images that played daily, was becoming overwhelming. An update on the local news reported that all leads were a dead end but the hotline will remain open. Such sad news, I had hoped they would have found him by now to give his parents closure and allow them to say their goodbyes with a proper burial. "Someone, please find this boy before I go mad!" I broke down and cried.

Suddenly, the images stopped in the middle of September and I had no idea why. A week later, the answer came. Preparing dinner, I turned on the news on the small portable TV in the kitchen. A wave went through me, and the image replayed in my mind. There was an update on the missing boy. Reporting he was found by hunters beside a farmer's field in the northeast of the city. His bike and backpack were found behind evergreens closer to the road.

They were investigating but believe the boy may have lost his way and climbed the tree to get his bearings. His injuries showed signs he fell out of the tree. I was stunned watching the footage taken from a helicopter. It was looking down and doing a half circle around the scene. The bare tree, the fence... the boy now covered with a sheet played out exactly like the mini-movie that haunted me for months.

I had to sit down to steady myself; I was shaking, tears running down my cheeks. Blessings to the hunters who found him, giving his parents the whereabouts and closure to ...

"Their Missing Boy."

21. The Doctors House

Some of my extended family lived in a very old-century home. It was a lovely brick house; they filled it with furniture to match the era of the house. There had been a lot of renovations by previous owners, some didn't make sense, and some were obviously needed. It had a lot of history, including the original owner, a doctor who practiced in the back part of the house.

The senior Lady of the house was always kind to me. I enjoyed our chit-chats out in the gardens, usually with a glass of red wine in hand. We often sat beside the long hedge of old-world roses; their scent was sweet and pleasant. Inside the house was a different story. It felt heavy and close, almost stagnate. You could feel it the minute you stepped in the door. At the time, I wasn't sure if it was the house or all those antique items that filled the rooms and walls.

One sunny afternoon, she took me around to an area at the back of the house and showed me a door. "Where does the door lead?" I asked. "I've not seen a door inside the house." She smiled and opened the door. It was a long, closed in hallway, almost the full width of the house. At the end of the hall was a door. I was surprised it led into the bathroom. I laughed, saying, "I thought this door was a linen closet!"

"I did too, until I went to fill it," she chuckled. "I have no idea why someone would wall in a hallway like that, but we will be removing the walls to gain more access to the foyer and kitchen." I agreed. To get to the kitchen from the living room, you had to go through the foyer and dining room. With the walls removed would end all that. Like I said, some of the renovations previous owners did, just didn't make sense. I noticed a remarkable change in the house, much lighter and airier after the renovations but there was something else. Feelings like you aren't alone.

I had recently acquired some old cast iron, so I inquired if she had any books I could borrow to help date the pieces. She went upstairs to have a look in the small library they had created in one of the spare bedrooms. As I sat in the dining room, I could hear her talking to herself. "Where is that book... I know it's here somewhere?" Within minutes, I heard her cry out, "Ouch... you didn't have to hit me on the head with it!" Knowing we were alone in the house I was confused. I sat at the table thinking over what I just heard, as I waited for her return.

Coming down the stairs, she was rubbing the top of her head. I asked her, "What happened? Are you all right?"

Somewhat chuckling she said, "This book fell off a top shelf and hit me right on top of my head!" Handing the book to me, it read Cast Iron Identification. It was exactly what I needed. The book had the information and pictures to be able to date or at least determine the circa of the pieces. I was still breezing through the pages when she returned with coffees.

"This is a great book, thank you. I'll get it back to you soon." She nodded as she sipped her coffee. "How's your head?" I asked.

"I'm okay but it really hurt when it happened." Rubbing the spot on her head, she leaned forward slightly in her chair. Her eyes squinting, she added, "Isn't that odd, the very book I was looking for fell and hit me on the head."

"Yes... very odd indeed." I mustered, sipping my coffee and breaking eye contact to end the conversation.

Visits were but a handful a year, but I couldn't help notice the house was becoming more active. Stories of odd events and creepy feelings were the topic of many conversations. For the most part I sat on the edge of the conversations unwilling to partake. I was sure the lady of the house was interacting with the activity. Who was I to put my 2 cents in with my opinion. The numerous things manifesting, could lead to problems in the future.

During one of those visits, I made the mistake of sitting in a chair at the opposite end of the long dining room table. Normally, I'd sit closest to the kitchen in order to be helpful. As I sat down I felt heaviness behind me, manifesting strong enough it felt like someone was standing behind the back of the chair. I froze not knowing what to expect, I waited... and then it happened. Out of nowhere the back of the chair shoved forward against my back jarring me. Two more shoves in a row was enough to make me stand up. I grabbed my purse and drink and sat at the other end of the table. Obviously, something didn't want me sitting there, I heeded the warning. At the time, I kept silent, never voicing what had happened.

One cold winter afternoon, we gathered in the living room to warm up in front of the wood stove. Slowly, the living room emptied, and I found myself sitting alone. I amused myself by scanning the room. There were collections everywhere, on the walls, cupboards, and shelves. The whole house was like taking a trip back in time. Noticing a small candle stick on the table beside me, I picked it up to look at the bottom. There was usually a tag with a date or circa. It read c1750s, I wasn't surprised. As I placed the candle stick down, the room suddenly became dense... heavy.

Transparent figures moved into the room, right through the wall. I had thought there must have been a door there at one time leading out to the back hallway that had been closed off. Perhaps the renovations stirred things up. Two men in suits and top hats moved behind the couch I was sitting on, a woman in a floor-length dress walked over and stood to my right. Two more women in similar period dresses, move through the wall into the living room and stood beside the woodstove. Although I couldn't hear them it was obvious they were talking amongst themselves.

At first, they didn't seem to notice me. I had thought what I was seeing was a glimpse of the past, until they all stopped and turned to look at me. Feeling surrounded and overwhelmed by them, I began to shake as the adrenaline started pumping through my body. My fight of flight response was kicking in. Getting up quickly, I left the room, seeking the company of the living.

After dinner, the kitchen was cleaned and dishes washed, the senior lady and I were sitting in our usual spot at the dining room table, sipping red wine. "You seem distracted or bothered by something; what's wrong?" she inquired. Not wanting to discuss what happened earlier, I decided to ask about the episode from my last visit.

"Who usually sits in the last chair at the other end of the table?" I blurted.

"My youngest daughter likes to sit there. She enjoys watching the birds at the feeder. Why do you ask?" she replied. I told her about the episode of the back of the chair being shoved. She told me, "Go sit there and let's see what happens."

I stared at her for a moment, finally saying, "I don't think that's a good idea."

"It will be fine," she said. "Come on now, you're brave." Against my better judgement, I complied and made my way down to the other end of the table. I turned and looked at her. She nods for me to go ahead. Slowly, I sat down, having trouble leaning back into the chair. Within a few minutes, I could feel a wall of pressure behind me, I sat forward.

"There is a woman behind you," the elderly lady said.

I replied, "I know, and she is not happy that I'm sitting here. I really don't think it's a good idea to provoke her!" I got up and returned to my seat. I could tell she was a little disappointed in me but I did what I felt comfortable with. That was the last time I visited...

"The Doctors House."

Author's Bio

Cent the Storyteller has had a lifelong interest in the odd, the unusual and the creepiness of the unexplained. For decades she has investigated these weird occurrences seeking knowledge and understanding. Always looking for a logical explanation, and when that fails, digging for old world knowledge and controversial theories. She forever searches for explanations of these weird occurrences.

A Life's Journey into the Paranormal Vol 1 is part of a collection created for her first book. These short stories were written to share these oddities that many others have experienced themselves.